Voyager

SRIKANTH REDDY

Voyager

 University of California Press   Berkeley   Los Angeles   London

NATIONAL ENDOWMENT FOR THE ARTS

This project is supported in part by an award from the National Endowment for the Arts.

University of California Press, one of the most distinguished university presses in the United States, enriches lives around the world by advancing scholarship in the humanities, social sciences, and natural sciences. Its activities are supported by the UC Press Foundation and by philanthropic contributions from individuals and institutions. For more information, visit www.ucpress.edu.

University of California Press
Berkeley and Los Angeles, California

University of California Press, Ltd.
London, England

LIBRARY OF CONGRESS CATALOGING-IN-PUBLICATION DATA

Reddy, Srikanth, 1973–.
  Voyager / Srikanth Reddy.
    p.   cm. — (New California poetry ; 31)
  ISBN 978-0-520-26885-2 (pbk. : alk. paper)
  1. Waldheim, Kurt—Poetry.   I. Title.
  PS3618.E427V69   2011
  811'.6—dc22   2010018492

Manufactured in the United States of America

20   19   18
10   9   8   7   6   5   4   3

The paper used in this publication meets the minimum requirements of ANSI/NISO Z39.48–1992 (R 1997) (Permanence of Paper).

For my father

~~Morti~~ li morti ~~e i vivi~~ parean vivi

PURGATORIO 12.67

.

Contents

BOOK ONE

The world is the world.

To deny it is to break with reason.

Nevertheless it would be reasonable to question the affair.

The speaker studies the world to determine the extent of his troubles.

He studies the night overhead.

He says therefore.

He says venerable art.

To believe in the world, a person has to quiet thinking.

The dead do not cease in the grave.

The world is water falling on a stone.

Some serve the state.

Some an interminable kingdom.

In the end he would have no objection to the study of nations.

Nations occur.

For a time, Finland.

Likewise, Namibia.

The Namibian people journey through the story of Namibia.

As a footnote, the Soviet Union is an interesting case.

He also will one day collapse.

A world is a world is a world.

Even so the world has to go on.

To complain about love in front of the famous Chagall window does not make a difference.

He shall be placed in the first circle.

The Chinese province of Sichuan continues to change form.

Subject the globe to assembly.

Mark in the empire thus.

[Figure 1].

In his mind he views a dark glass sea.

Before diving in he talks of dialectical space.

Jerusalem. Jerusalem indeed.

Is is.

There is no distinction between ideology and image.

One.

He records his name on a gold medallion.

Two.

The philosopher must say is.

The world is legion.

The self is a suffering form.

Is is.

Waves rise and fall, but the sea remains.

Open the box.

No.

The box is a brief history of post-war Europe.

Opening it would be against the interests of the authorities.

They could bring influence to bear on a man.

De facto world.

Black palace.

One would not wish this account to become a catalogue of the disappeared.

Disappearance should not fashion books.

Aldo Moro found in the boot of a parked car is the great private work of nations.

If there is a story, it is this.

He had a professorship at the university and had been out of contact with his personality as a result.

His parting words made mention of the dark work of fact.

Fact is the script of the unknown.

Its shadowy disclosure documents the further world.

And was he some obscure thwarted figure in byzantine constraints?

The question arose.

He knew the topography of injustice.

It had neither inside nor outside, like love.

Like a long ago fire in the world.

War is.

War is a failure of form.

Thus sink each day's dead softly in the hearth.

Some suffer within flagrant circles.

Some take refuge in the avenues of the cross.

He was seeking an interpretation of *arms and the man* that would not further legitimize the regime.

Autumn was in pieces all across America.

Death may be a change of style, but surely not of substance.

There there.

The river lives in a mobile home.

Is desire present throughout the line?

Yes she said.

He said the final object is the cross.

Is the world one muted figure cut down with hands tied?

Carry out the bodies.

The body in the line means little.

Weigh voice.

Namibia Namibia Namibia Namibia.

Within seeds, increase.

Within uncertainty, understanding.

The failed idea repeatedly described in this book is *alter ego*.

On the shield, endless ranges beyond an agricultural field, and an observer there, regarding it all in perspective.

Peace. Peace.

One.

The sovereign subject thinking of time reasons accordingly.

One. One. Two. One.

Constraint fathers compulsion.

Do the dead work beyond sense?

Say creature into the mirror.

If the image displeases, the remedy does not lie in shattering the mirror.

On stage, the Cold War.

To the west, the canal moving through the corridors of a burning former capital.

Critics should take into account the function of repetition in disciplined states of mind.

Peace. Peace.

Picture the deep sea bed.

Is the sea crafted by the will to believe?

The enlightened believe.

They live together in a village in history.

Seven. Six. Five.

The flames continued until a world appeared.

He wrote formally in private.

Vote for a.

Make wings of straw.

Vote for the.

Everybody say servant in the cross.

Thanks be to the university research professor for diplomacy.

Is is a number?

Enter one.

Österreich ist eine kleine Welt, in der die Große ihre Probe hält.

A is the ground for the.

On a cold winter's day, a pack of porcupines huddled together seeking refuge from the frost.

Soon they had to move apart again as their quills struck home.

Need drew them together.

They found themselves repelled by stabs of pain.

Thus in his fable Schopenhauer the German philosopher describes unending peace.

Approach the pendulum.

There is a school of thought that sees constraint as the basis of relations with other people.

The book of the is taken apart and put together again with relation to a.

Over the centuries the oceans have remained unshattered.

The good interpreter shifts ever on.

One.

He is fashioned in the assembly of his book.

One.

Kurt Waldheim is a formal negotiation.

One.

A collective music circles history.

One.

The world is the largest picture in the world.

One.

Of the individual, only a number remains.

Death is a little door in the world.

Vis pacem.

The star systems pace in perception.

Process. Blind process.

The nature of systems is now becoming clear.

The world is a world.

Overcome all emotion.

Wherever possible alleviate the misery of others.

There is nothing in victory.

The silent alone lie united.

BOOK TWO

In November last year, I became interested in the fate of a machine which had been launched into creation and disappeared from sight during my boyhood. The thought of it roaming our system unconcerned about the policies of the regime was a relief from the strains and suspicions that surrounded us at home. Every morning, I would visit the library to dig out information for my dissertation on the principles of writing, and in the night, overhead, sought refuge in the parallel journey.

Aboard, I read, was a deeply-etched record of the world that floated away, full of popular tunes and beautiful technological problems. Perhaps an observer far in outer space might study this information in days to come. He would have to weigh carefully in his heart the words of a man who by some quirk of fate had become a spokesman for humanity, who could give voice to all the nations and peoples of the world, and, so to speak, the conscience of mankind.

This man, legend states, likely knew of the mass execution of groups of people as a capable officer required to collect and analyze data, prepare reports, conduct investigations, and otherwise facilitate operational projects in the last world war. At the time, however, he did not express concern at this action. To a degree this is understandable. His voice failed. Now, after years have passed, our little record is carrying his words as Secretary General of the United Nations to a government above.

Thus I built up a dossier about him over a considerable period of time. His story cast a shadow of unreality over everything. The summer heat relentlessly continued. At home, my wife sent for a parcel of china that one day will come. Whether this will happen in the far distant future I cannot predict. Certainly the china plays no part in the tribulations of the last year.

Even if he had intelligence of disquieting matters, I do not wish to judge here the person of Dr. Waldheim. The dead do not cease in the grave. The world is water falling on a stone. True, I began to cross out words from his book on world peace. But I had mixed emotions about this new development in my life. As a child, spelling out *world* was to open a world in myself, private and byzantine, with mountains by a pale, fragile sea, the coast stretching southwards in the curtained evening hours. Now, to cross line after line out of his work seemed to me a slow and difficult process that verged on the ridiculous.

I labored, often tempted to throw up my hands in frustration, on this form. I expunged colonial wars, the Cape Verde Islands, the dilemma of self, and a broken government thus. Within a year, the little declarations that remained seemed to me to silence any hope for a united world. *Nations occur. / For a time, Finland. / Likewise, Namibia. / The Namibian people journey through the story of Namibia. / As a footnote, the Soviet Union is an interesting case. / He also will one day collapse . . .*

In my office a globe was set up, less a world than a history of imperialism and corruption. I used to search that poor political patchwork in the period leading up to my tenure. As a scholar, it became obvious to me that my little book would be unsuccessful. I had no reason for undertaking this form. But the thought of making a new beginning started to operate on me in the midst of Spring. In Austria, obviously ill and depressed, the Secretary General survived the turmoil within, with considerable reserve. I had to cross his world out anew. This history is the effect of that curious process.

On the Indian sub-continent, a prince was isolated from all knowledge that might upset him. In the palace he began to lament his captivity. *Could this self, born in a stream of sad time, only be makeshift? I consider my position over and over. In ships, the sea is law. In famine, the field.* Therefore he took the occasion to visit the country. *My my,* he said, *I understand nothing.* The map of Asia was in the making during this period. Serious political disturbances were causing people to flee warfare, drought and famine. Some thrust aside their tragedies to cope. *The self in theory is a problem. The word does not even cover the remains.*

If there is a story, it is this. At one point I had tears in my eyes. Now I consider the light of morning in a major university, reflecting on the failure of reason in *Alice in Wonderland*. Each week, I plan an assignment. *Students, interrogate form down to the last comma. Students, broadcast the crimes of history.* In March, the government, mired once again in a morass of confusion and double-dealing, had no way of explaining American casualties in the war. It had neither inside nor outside, like a long ago fire in the world.

The history of Iraq developed long ago, along the confluence of the Tigris and Euphrates rivers. The Ottoman Empire followed years later. In Baghdad, the formalized line in the Persian fashion deteriorated when the Arab world appeared to dissolve in turmoil and disorganization. So, for some Iraqis, silence became a figure for the infinite. Thus sink each day's dead softly in the hearth. The china, meanwhile, approached home, but not directly, and in pieces.

I had started Tolstoi's *War and Peace* on a number of occasions, and was much moved by his understanding of nations, foreign policy, and many other realms. But I have to say that it is interminable. Sometimes a work is clarified by ironies, as in the scene of complete disarray during which the troops go in the river with their heavy equipment, and substantial casualties result among the French within minutes. As I write these lines, people with pictures of fighters killed in action run through New York's traffic-choked streets, rising to the spirit of the occasion, while I, sitting in my second-floor office connected to various communications cables, maintain control over some very unruly emotional forces.

To me, the people on the roadside waving placards and banners appeared to be immobilized, without force, and, paradoxically, representative of *our troops*. It was difficult to see how to stop the activities of the government. I had an essential volume which touched upon the question of autonomy, a copy out of our library. I studied it carefully, surprised by the extent to which political philosophy was marked by faith. The style, formal and cool, highlighted the limitations of feeling. In my office I would often consider that bleak voice, convinced that, in the end, it was a splendid lamentation.

To cross scenes out of a text would not be to reject the whole text. Rather, to cross out a figure such as *to carry out* ~~programmes they approve~~ *the* ~~various regional economic commissions and inter-governmental~~ *bodies* sometimes increases the implications. I had hoped to voice my unhappiness in the world thus. More and more, it seems to me the role of the Secretary General in this book is that of an *alter ego*. In a nightmare, Under Secretaries General, Assistant Secretaries General, and other officials of rank reported directly to me. I was given an office and a globe. But I wondered why the forest just beyond the window seemed so cold when it was, to be sure, rapidly burning.

In the flames I distinguished many strange and ambiguous forms. But I remained among the voluminous archives. I had to write my memoirs in German—*Ist Welt die Probe?*—again and again. Elsewhere in the darkness, a messianic little devil was screaming *The world is constraint* as the words that I wrote were taken apart and put together again, this time as a study of John 2:1. This subconscious vision has shaken my view of the world as singular. So I silence myself in a book of the *a*. Kurt Waldheim is a formal negotiation. A collective music circles history.

In the ruined remains of the china, one can discern a figured individual in the background of a far field. I have seen him with his basket of soil, a private man, stocky, with a manner that makes conversation an effort. Bridges to the East. I was intrigued by a sentimental touch in the image. In the office I had ample opportunity to observe this piece, obsessed by the idea that it was a figure for life on our planet, which, having reached the abyss of immeasurable outer space, has now come to Earth.

Now I realize that, in the theatres of neutrality, the heart freezes. This is a difficult problem. Everybody watches the wheel as it turns. Apparently incapable of peace and well-being, and unable to draw political conclusions, in the late summer, on the outskirts of a small town to the south, I embraced a new work. It was engendered in my dream. It was built of desire. Experience taught me that, in the final analysis, nothing ends. The first steps must follow.

BOOK THREE

I

It was a forlorn eve,
        my descent wintry.
                In that foreign midnight,

I sounded
        the chanceries of doubt
            as day drove up

in an ordinary yellow cab.
        To my astonishment,
            I seemed to be blindfolded

but the clock
       —talk   talk—
           continuing called me,

a voice ever stranger
        in complaint.
           With my staff I came

to the first step,
        sanguine indeed,
           and dressed in a well-cut Western suit

—quite the best I saw on anybody
                during my whole stay
                                in that unstable regime.

There were people in plots
                bowing to creation.
                                Please I protested,

I had not come to stay.
                You will go in

                                said Nobody,

all will be quiet.
                I looked down

                                and could see thousands

crowding into the grounds
                —my   my—

                                and climbed into the burial site.

Within the twisted
                rows of graves,

                                the teeth of under,

some spoke of hatred
  and some of hope.
        Blind, they wept on command,

in wheelchairs,
    on crutches,
        waving stumps.

It was rather haunting—
    the gate of shadows,
        the path unlit,

and ahead,
    also dark,
        an abandoned fortress.

Carried along by the crowd,
    our way lit by flashlights
        through dim corridors,

I said *Citizens,*
    no   *no.*
        Ahead, a door opened.

I recognized the old council
        sitting round a table,
                some in religious collars,

the atmosphere a court.
        Chairing the proceeding,
                a tall, bearded figure

uttered a few words in German
        for my benefit.
                He had lived for a time

and remarked
        that I needed
                to be *dealt with.*

Listening quietly,
        I tried to avoid
                any show of emotion.

This clearly displeased him.
        He seemed to expect me
                to present my own commentary.

I said in reply
       the following,
              shaken and uneasy,

the slim thread of truth but little help . . .

2

I was born into empire,
    my crown in poor condition.
        A world broke out,

a world drained of weather.
    Mother made me
        from whatever little was available,

a window,
    a magnet—
        my   my,

I remembered my life—
    my father nothing more
        than footsteps in a clinic.

War broke out one day.
    It sickened me to see such slaughter,
        but I liked horses and rank

which led to the army.
    To the Far Front
        we were called,

and marched
　　　　　into newsreel footage
　　　　　　　　　without a word—

I continued in Latin,
　　　　although they made a point
　　　　　　　　of stopping me frequently,

under constant surveillance
　　　　in that plot we all shared.
　　　　　　　　We were surrounded—

a squadron of horse,
　　　　a squadron of bicycles,
　　　　　　　　another of motorized weather.

When the rains came,
　　　　the call came to fire.
　　　　　　　　It was desperate work,

a passport to heaven.
　　　　Wounded by a splinter,
　　　　　　　　a serious wound,

by happy chance
        mein lieber Freund,
                I was evacuated,

my regiment disbanded,
        and in a little train
                listening to the countryside

I prayed somehow
        in a cattle wagon
                perched on a crate of apples.

Along the line we stopped
        at innumerable stations
                whose names we could not read.

We never stopped crying "No."
        Later we reached my house,
                the windows blown out,

winter hard by and the farm for sale.

3

In that dream
            born of the wretchedness
                        etched in identity,

I broke down
            and was called
                        into the office of a minister.

He had held the job
            since the election of man,
                        a clandestine Christian

with a gift for friendship.
            He said *Waldheim,*
                        I believe I believe,

therefore I believe.
            That venerable form,
                        subtle in art,

with cold ruined hand
            had written a book
                        which caused uproar in Eden.

Lower,

       look lower.

              You speak of reality

under illusions

       in an earthy little world turning.

           ~~John 1:4~~

However perhaps

       accompanied by me

              the Minister went on,

through worlds beyond reason

       an adventure in the unreal

              might be of interest?

Given the circumstances,

       I whispered

              There must be some mistake,

I am not expecting any call.

       By now the Minister

              was going through my portfolio,

and, moved by goodwill,
              he commented that the caviar tin
                    on the table

had been handed
              to Saint Bruno
                    after their work in Italy.

I became red
              —not in connection with the heat,
                    just touched by this gesture—

and told him I could not imagine a better job.

4

Drawing to a close,
   he was quiet—

      so I said my name

from time to time
   and wondered

      whether I sounded

like myself.
   The Minister

      pointed out a little book.

Looking at the strange pictures—
   a black sun,

      the Earth seen from inside,

and war in a box—
   My my,

      such pictures!

A little gallery of being
   I thought,

      but soon found

unending regions
        of consequence
                under every image

—fields endless
        but visible
                behind every field.

So I and the Minister
        left for a quest
                under this world,

thus seeking
        to return home
                in new country,

our little joke being
        We don't believe
                we're making believe—

star fields
        prevailing in the East
                over the kingdom

as a man considered a pile of bones.
        There he was,
                blunt Under,

resigned to his post—
        a loyal servant
                of the world above.

Under had been serving
        for some time
                and had served perfectly well,

but now
        he had perhaps
                drunk a glass too many,

as he was known to do on occasion,
        for somewhere in the mountains
                his wife was looking into her hands

to see once more where Under lived.
        In a soft voice he explained
                he could no longer return

to his wife and daughter,
        because Under now served
                in nations of continual shadow.

This beguiling man
        said *Death is another home,*
                smiling at my problems

with the world in general,
        and particularly personality
                —that foreign little whole—

which he advised me to bury completely.

5

Lost in the middle of life
                we continued.
                                It seemed essential

to build a house.
                Clouds were gathering.
                                They perturbed the Minister.

He complained
                that I did not believe
                                in his extraordinary world.

I saw him quiet
                those who refused him—
                                their heads in a privy,

saying *Waldheim,*
                we believe we do not believe ...
                                I could not accept

that they were so many,
                and was overcome
                                on the banks of the canal.

The dead do not cease in the grave
                    I wrote on a stone
                                  as the Minister,

his voice running out,
                    said *Either go back*
                              or move forward by other means ...

Colleagues, I had done some thinking
                    about Genesis 1:2
                              and was becoming emotional

so yes, I followed him
                    with reddish eyes,
                              a man of words.

Finally the road stopped—
                    the untoward road,
                              the road made of blood—

and in the light of the fire
                    continuing forward
                              I approached a closed door in the field.

Not of this world,
        it nevertheless remained
                substantially in place—

stationed in the ruins
        of a great stage
                under nations.

Opening that door,
        I now looked on a dim room
                with one empty chair.

In the opposing chair,
        broken King If said
                Sit down with me.

In his office
        under the world,
                he expressed concern

at my desire for illusions.
        Help me I said.
                There was a book

in the office

        that I wished to view—

                new within

but old without—

        In the Middle ~~East~~ of life

            it more or less went,

unthinkable to the end.

6

My   my
>   Archbishop A
>>   with his deteriorating wing

regarded the world.
>   I visited the spirit
>>   there in his august palace.

He complained about the heat
>   and asked if I would mind
>>   if he took his mitre off.

I agreed and took off my coat.
>   Whether he really believed
>>   is difficult to say ...

Certainly life
>   burned inside him.
>>   He had composed a few lines

in Greek,
>   insisting it was only a draft.
>>   *My shaky work* he called it,

but I had to admire the line
            There   there.
                        In Greek I repeated it.

He would look
            into the blue overhead
                        from this private chamber

and praise his own words
            with no intention
                        whatsoever to stop.

Very little could be done,
            so I took it upon myself
                        as cautiously as possible

to cross that phantom out thus
            ~~Archbishop A~~
                        and took the chair

there   there
                in disrepair.
                        There was an eerie silence

at the table.
        I tried making
                stone men to continue

the discussion.
        As evening progressed,
                the men unbent—

Good
        edging closer
             good   *good* . . .

We spent hours discussing forms.
        One had a map of the real
                that we later published

in the *Times* in Latin.
        One opened a little clock
                and said *freedom.*

Together
        we opened my will
                over August wine

poured into new bottles
               as one asked

                          Why don't you smile?

I smiled, and set my spade by.

7

Given early baptism
      in a grave
           as the Minister described

creation and the fall,
      I found fences
           all laid down in blood.

How
      I cannot say—
           they were broken in unity,

deteriorated unity.
      Thus continuing,
           we looked with little reason

for peace
      in utterly black country.
           Time had affected the stability

of the western steps.
      ~~step~~   ~~step~~
           I had to speak

to deny silence,

        and proclaimed *I believe*

                —my frosty speech white

in the atmosphere.

        My   my,

                I was happy

to see peaceful Escher

        in that territory

                recording the view.

As a whole

        Escher's world

                was mine—

old Escher

        with his failed heart

                like a toothless bulldog

following the lines

        drawn by the world,

                an aggregation of white

dominated by black.
   Young friend

       he said,

formal objectivity
    might be

       a personal matter—

and finally the view,
    whole and fair,

       appeared,

a demilitarized zone
    extending on both sides

       in which further illusions were salvaged.

I took the chair
    under the umbrella

       and saw a train journey

through the countryside
    on the approach

       to a further world.

Alive while burning,
> *Sir* I called,

>> *I would take soundings Sir ...*

In the chaos,
> an ample ivory villa
>> was open to faith.

I have seen the ruins
> —the white black,
>> the black white—

but a man cannot live there.

8

I was led to a globe,
            beholden

                        to its vast revolution

—a revolution living eyes
            could hardly credit—

                        my life diminishing in scale,

myself the moving woods
            they called *the real,*

                        guided by a spirit

to low countries in disarray.
            The patchwork of views

                        emerged in negative—

machinery in the fields,
            ground work,

                        the promise of form

in the background.
            There was a universal man,
                        a scholar of history.

To exercise his heart,
>>he would complain about love
>>>>in front of the famous Chagall window—

autumn,
>>that revision of the year,
>>>>covering the ground;

one swallow
>>moving south;
>>>>form working the levers—

and I became a disciple of despair,
>>for I had a long good look at that world.
>>>>*Help* I said.

In the first circle,
>>the centre of never,
>>>>the Minister had constructed a residence

which included a private zoo
>>where he kept a collection
>>>>of exotic political leaders

set in the midst of vineyards,
               the surrounding waters deep,
                             his great concern

the erosion under the world.
               Greeting me there
                           with dinner in mind,

he launched his primitive harpoon
               at men in the dark.
                           One gargled and spat,

then he swallowed the skin
               red and raw,
                           which he insisted

was the best way
               to eat a respected
                           former Congressman.

Well,
               very well . . .
                         It was an old

and somewhat shabby-looking Falcon
        professing disbelief—
                Are you thing

or king?
        I was impressed by the speech
                (hard indeed to respond),

and facing him I said *Help.*
        He was co-operative,
                and over that Sahara within

he invited me to cross
        beyond the fragile coast
                towards the wisest men.

Friends,
        somewhat surprised
                by grace I was flown

to universal applause
        —from the West
                to the East summoned—

asking the Minister,
                    my speech in disarray,
                                    Is that legion I see

hitherto doomed?
                    climbing higher
                                    as new countries approached,

taken up
                    in the still atmosphere
                                    and weighed down

by an increasing mood of *If only* ...

9

This is the universal journey
        the gravest proclaimed
                in a universal language

on a universal stage,
        but I found the sound
                of hunger in the background

rather distressing.
        Picture the scene.
                Aged women accused their world

in unison,
        the refrain quiet.
                I approached with my list of names.

Before me
        a figure said *No,*
                waving a white handkerchief

and dancing.
        (That lady, dancing,
                seemed to me a delicate shape

held under breaking ice).
            The aged Minister,
                        courteous but intractable,

invited me to make a speech
            in that envisaged theatre.
                        My somewhat nebulous host,

his head a needless conference of wounds,
            showed little interest
                        in my list of fellow religionaries

as I called *Release them,*
            at pains to say *Please,*
                        for I worried about fate,

if I could bear it,
            and a man with a halo,
                        black toga billowing,

invited me to listen
            to the heart
                        I wish I had in life—

Death,

       death ...

            I had the highest regard for him.

(I spoke a little Italian,

       and was reading

           his *Tragedy of Aldo Moro*—

in Italian it was

       most moving).

           With his staff he went

into his white house.

       We were ushered in

           and said *world* in different ways.

I was impressed by his interest

       in my work—

           he tried to encourage me,

comparing his with my own,

       and made a moving speech

           on one man's faltering steps

towards the hard barren ground of human suffering ...

10

On the Indian sub-continent,
　　　　a prince was isolated
　　　　　　　from all knowledge

that might upset him.
　　　　In the palace he began
　　　　　　　to lament his captivity—

"Could this self,
　　　　born in a stream of sad time,
　　　　　　　only be makeshift?

I consider my position
　　　　over and over.
　　　　　　　In ships, the sea is law.

In famine, the field."
　　　　Therefore he took the occasion
　　　　　　　to visit the country.

"My my" he said,
　　　　"I understand nothing."
　　　　　　　The map of Asia was in the making

during this period.
　　　　Serious political disturbances
　　　　　　　　were causing people to flee

warfare,
　　　　　drought,
　　　　　　　　and famine.

Some thrust aside
　　　　their tragedies to cope.
　　　　　　　　"The self in theory is a problem.

The word does not even cover the remains."

II

My   my,
          I had no inkling
                    of the crowds within,

and considered every avenue
          which might lead
                    to enlightenment.

On the first step I called
          with tears in my eyes
                    —(that is poetic license,

it is not easy for me to cry)—
          No

                    no . . .

A Byzantine Ambassador appeared.
          That plucked out émigré of quiet—
                    I wondered what lay behind his words.

Perhaps you would permit me
          revealingly he said
                    a little scenario?

This all seemed to me
        to have a distinct
                Alice in Wonderland quality.

Nevertheless the Ambassador
        outlined the plan
                of a public performance.

White was his wing
        working in the dark
                as I listened with increasing doubt

to this elaborate script.
        It was extremely complicated
                —full of traps I could not see—

but I agreed to play my part.
        My role was to speak
                to Mohammed the Revolutionary.

Under the world
        that able guide awaited,
                intent on the secret of everything.

True form
              he hinted,
                        setting up a little house of cards,

never promises to remain.
               I suggested that we be off
                     and thus left,

a post-mortem figure
               in byzantine constraints
                     discussing the real

with everyone I met
               at the funeral of fact.
                     Mohammed complained

of injustice,
               turning from the world,
                     and called for vengeance

against fate.
               Consequently,
                     I consulted his book

which I was told
            in Teheran
                        had performed well.

It had neither inside
            nor outside,
                        like ~~holy~~

~~War~~
            love
                        —its fabric absence.

Friends,
            possessed of a clear mind,
                        if not happy,

he spoke on the erosion of wisdom.
            I liked him,
                        his rage at spiritual irony,

his mastery of perhaps,
            his head removed in the field
                        by the American people—

is that history?

12

In the middle of that failed regime
            I made a fire.
                        A messianic peacock appeared.

I must have looked surprised,
            for, whirling, he said
                        Slogans   slogans . . .

So I in silence
            regarded the fire.
                        It was a loophole in time,

a detailed plan
            of the the.
                        The Minister contented himself

with listening to the fire—
            that indefatigable flag,
                        that red question we faced.

Distracted in the house,
            the growing frostiness
                        seemed to make the distance watchful.

The eye does not lie.
Some form continues
and will continue.

Thus the flames,
countless and imponderable,
sink anew—

solved,
whole,
~~Holy~~.

13

Time crackled softly
            in the hearth.
                        The world the world he said

and nodded gravely.
            I asked whether
                        there was any message

he wanted me to convey.
            Leaning back in his chair,
                        stony and objective,

the Minister gripped a letter
            concerning friendship,
                        good neighbourliness,

and co-operation
            between the Democratic Republic
                        of Union

and the International Committee
            of the Non-Aligned Movement
                        for Foreign Community,

which united

        this world

                with the other—

but friends,

        I rejected the text.

                Sir, I formally object

on matters of substance

        I said

                (for we had become

mere puppets in a scene

        from Chapter 2

                of Tolstoi's *War and Peace*),

slowly and with difficulty,

        since I do not speak Russian

                and could do little but say

do svidanya,

        walking towards a succession

                of old men from Moscow—

the old guard,

        the outspoken

                ambassadors there,

brilliant delegates

        who,

                in a friendly spirit,

dwelt at some length

        on the making of the key

                that opens the quiet,

turning in the mechanics of fact ...

14

I was troubled
        by the quiet
                river of illusion.

Only self could move
        that heavy river,
                which turned on its way.

We remained
        in place of course,
                and suffered changes,

and finally arrived.
        I had to build
                the Minister a fire,

and even though
        he did not feel that fire,
                it was my Jerusalem.

We halted for the night
        in a gloomy mood
                down the road

from the Palace of Un.
                    Our welcome took place
                                    in an austere room

decorated only with a few pictures.
                    Un said
                                    (without actually saying so)

that one represented
                    The Liberation of Palestine.
                                    It was a little prospect,

morning somewhere,
                    and hotel beds
                                    in the garden.

When I jokingly asked him
                    how he liked beds,
                                    the spirit assured me

he had slept a long time.
                    Ahead, the floor
                                    was under assembly.

Steps hurried down
        to a small podium where
                connected to various cables

I was to remain—
        while before the cameras,
                Un, that intriguing character

(unshaven,
        unruly,
             and formal)

asked why I denied
        the play of perceptions.
                I repeated *my my,*

inspected my fly,
        and made gestures
             towards the ground.

There, under the future,
        I saw Hamlet
             in a mobile home.

I called on him
        to stop his complaints,
                my hand on his various wing.

He had a volume
        which he studied carefully
                and, though weary and depressed,

I heard him utter his tragic history
        with coffee and cakes
                by the promised sea.

He said
        Perhaps
                my problem is action,

and I had to agree.
        He had come to see
                the play as a failure,

a general calamity
        in five episodes.
                In that lost Globe,

the bleak critics regarded it
        as a base failure.
                My own position in this matter

has long been clear
        —for I condone the implantation
           of form

in form—
        and within the play
            I also put a play,

and it is all action.

15

[a splendid

lamentation]

[under *constraints*

the

scarred
form

steps
in]

~~act~~

~~two~~

[He

                        bolts

his

     quiet

       sovereign

       to

       a cross]

          [Assembly
        of the globe]

[Because

    visits

                       him

                in the little

      chamber]

                   [he

  points

                to

          a   *text*

under

the

world]

            [the   scale
                    levels]

~~act~~

                    ~~one~~

                    [they
                    cut

down

> *the*

> > *body]*

[What

> *comes*

> > *in]*

> *[a succession of ambassadors]*

[need

> *without]*

[Horatio

      the

        voice

    of
unhappiness

     acting

       up

        a

    little]

[Assembly

                of the
              Other]

                   [voting

                            beyond]

              [Egypt
magnified]

[But

              the   Sea

    continues

within]

[The
mouth
of

the
Secretary
working
hard]

[The
ceiling

suffering   stress]

[repeatedly

forcing the   *hand*
through higher
levels]

[The

book

endlessly

Changes]

[In

a

nightmare

the

Given

appears]

[they are
United

in   autumn]

[Office

work

beyond]

[He

types   perhaps]

[They

Minister

in

The
field]

[making   *a*
negative]

[they   *part*

Without]

16

I tried to cut through
        all our hurried centuries,
                lost in a forest within.

Men
        broken by war
                emerged in frightful shape—

more than human
        but also less,
                they were quite aware,

the sovereign dead,
        that time is like a window
                opening up the sad patterns of never.

As one they advanced—
        ~~Lloyd George~~
            ~~Georges Clemenceau~~

~~Adolph Hitler~~
        —through history.
           But the past does not follow

101

so straightforward a path
    said I

        (predictably in Italian),

and, burning

     under their masters,
       they proclaimed

the world a pendulum.
     It is possible,

       but this gives rise

to the often-heard complaint
     that repetition is unavoidable.
       Still time issues into today,

little fathers.
    The years, I believe,
       can be shaped with one's hands.

The world
    —its obscure moving fields,
      Persian tragedies,

and countries in peace—
        I had to inform
                that council of the lost,

remains an instrument,
        a valve instrument,
                which, when waning,

is perfectly clear in the pit
        —and, being given
                to such classical concepts

as freedom and necessity,
        laboriously continued
                in the traditional way—

I believe ~~*I believe*~~.

17

Stripped of illusions
        on the wheel of innumerable I
            ~~my~~   ~~my~~

in the flames,
        friends and colleagues,
            I distinguished the summit

of the tabled world.
        It was a happy time—
            a time I bear in mind,

for now the Minister
        was a pure formality.
            I put an old shoe on

and, arriving in autumn thus,
        in excellent health,
            at the summit started looking

through bush and stone
        for further instructions in Latin.
            There above all

it appeared to be warm,
        but I felt a certain coolness
                when I decided to remove my name

formally.
        There there,
             nothing personal—

on his manoeuvring wings
        Prince Also,
              the straw fellow,

studied the atmosphere.
        He evidently found it cold too,
              and as a symbol of his friendship

asked me into the chapel
        to check through voluminous archives
              taken from nations.

I started to write my memoirs,
        the old fringe of world
              become a centre

in which I moved.
                    One of my last acts
                                   was the transfer of the works east.

This was essential
                    because of the constraints it imposed
                                   on the West.

It was happy hour
                    for the next thousand years.
                                   Freed from burden

in the elder kingdom,
                    the former world set
                                   beyond the West—

as the playwright ~~Hebbel~~ once wrote,
                    Ist eine kleine Welt
                                   in der die große ihre Probe hält?

A is the ground for the.

18

On a cold winter's day,
　　　　a pack of porcupines huddled close
　　　　　　　　seeking refuge from the frost.

Soon however
　　　　they had to move apart,
　　　　　　　　their home being pain.

Thus in his fable
　　　　~~Schopenhauer~~
　　　　　　　　the philosopher describes

(albeit unintentionally)
　　　　my emotions
　　　　　　　　on the train back again.

I recall a playground
　　　　in open country,
　　　　　　　　the sudden upsurge

of a building—
　　　　little perceptions
　　　　　　　　travelling the Union lines

to the conclusion within—
        strange with wisdom,
                to say nothing of

the messianic sense of Paine.
        It was cold
                in that tragically designed

techno-scientific vehicle of self,
        a devil screaming in pursuit
                The world is constraint.

Thinking of Professor F,
        the grand old man,
                I opened his book on union.

This book,
        taken thoroughly apart
                and put together again

with relation to me,
        soon came unstuck—
                whereupon it proved impossible

to obtain any understanding of
~~John 2:1~~

union.

Deep down, citizens,
without wishing to set myself up
as a psychiatrist, I am convinced

that subconscious oceans
unshattered in the early years
promise a return to former union

one said.
It was Margaret,
the ardent believer,

hammering down the issue.
We should believe she said,
for the only way out

is to accept this world . . .
So facing the countries I had left,
with the East in view

as Christian
        and Furthermore
                renewed their quarrels,

I avoided speaking
        in my unhappy state,
                overcome by glory—

whereupon Silence leant across
        and asked whether I would be good
                enough to man the wheel.

(I consider him my maker,
        and thus was disposed
                to maintain good relations).

With the utmost courtesy,
        I   ~~Kurt Waldheim~~
                frowned at the view

—the river sparkling outside,
        a man delivering a sofa,
                the high echelons of the saved,

and the moribund
        unhappy queues
                of generations who faded

~~generation~~
        ~~generation~~
            to the West

throughout history,
        ruined utterly I believe,
            moving still

over prosperous empires
        one after another—
            blind people that see,

~~I believe~~
        seeking a way
            without even a measure of identity

yet at home in the remains.
        I have seen that living line of people
           turning with time

on bridges to the East.
                    They have gone far
                                        with their replica virgin and child.

However,
              the Union Central
                              finally left that country's people

who long to come in
                    —*nobody in,*

                              everybody in—

Death opening the door.

19

Drawn in outer space
            on a ceiling of night,
                        a hinged balance held true.

That balance
            —its mechanisms
                      worked into the unknown—

emerged
            in the star systems
                      which turn in union

without history
            as we know it
                  on this planet.

I recognize it
            to the East
                  said I to the West,

not made,
            not given,
                  over the world.

Devoted observers,
    it seems to me
        a just structure.

~~John 1:5~~
    And my search
        for peace underground

now come to an end
    —constraints accepted
        in spirit as well as in letter,

the line spent,
    the theatres in abandon—
        I viewed the balances

more clearly than ever before.

~~Epilogue~~

I stood before the remains of the war,
        whistling
                until a door opened within

my life.
        My   my,
                what guided me through?

No answer
        can be given.
                However, I feel my study of conscience

engendered in me that dream
        which showed me
                a small tempered globe.

Nowhere have I found another
        of that material.
                There is nothing stronger.

Yet I am not without hope,
        citizens.
                I am a believer in silent prayers

relinquished.

EPILOGUES

Epilogue

In the late summer of 1945, on the outskirts of a small town to the south of Vienna, my wife, my infant daughter Liselotte and I stood before the gutted remains of my parents' house. The war was over at last and, after countless trials and tribulations, we refugees had found our way home from the Austrian Alps. Our quest, however, was not yet over: we sought not only our parents but also a roof over our heads.

The appearance of my parents' house dashed all our hopes: a ruin scorched by fire with the wind whistling at will through the broken window-panes. Utterly dejected and in silence we crept around the garden to the back, convinced that nobody could be living within the shattered walls—until suddenly we heard voices, and a door opened. Within seconds we were being embraced by my father and mother: both had survived the war.

Forty years have passed since that day, which, after years of dictatorship and military service, marked for me the start to a new life, a life that at the outset had been filled with insecurity and anxiety about our future—a life that had also been marked by tragic events and experiences that were to determine my future thoughts and actions.

Many years later, after I had been elected by the United Nations to the highest office that the international community can bestow, I was repeatedly asked: where—behind all the impartiality of the office—were my real roots? Which principles had governed my life and work? What had guided me along the lonely path through the undergrowth of ideologies and vested interests?

Like all essential questions, no simple answer can be given. In retrospect, however, I feel that certain decisive influences can be traced: the history of Europe, my continent, and Austria, my homeland; my bitter experience of war; my study of law and my diplomatic career; as well as my

belief in democracy and the tenets of Christianity. Together they helped
me to observe the claims of my conscience amidst all the different and often
conflicting advice submitted by my international advisers.

It was the tragic involvement of Europe in two world wars that
engendered in me, as in so many of its citizens, the hope that national
power politics could be overcome, and gave birth to my dream of a supra-
national world government.

It was Austria's indefatigable will to recover, and its active policy of
neutrality, which showed me and my countrymen what solidarity and
hard work can achieve and how bridges can be built between neighbours,
however different their ideological concepts might be.

It was the war, with its hecatombs of innocent victims and ravages of
minds and material, that convinced me of just how much men and women
all over the world cherish one common desire: peace and security for
themselves and their children.

It was my study of law that brought home to me the degree to which a
peaceful family of nations is dependent upon the existence and observance
of mutually accepted norms as well as upon an international mechanism
for solving conflict.

It was in my diplomatic career, through which I had always hoped to
contribute in some small way to furthering understanding between
peoples and nations, that I learnt to overcome distrust and scepticism
through personal contacts and patient dialogue free of all emotion

It was allegiance to democracy, tempered by the experience of fascism,
which taught me that in the final analysis nothing is weaker than
dictatorship. During my countless journeys around the globe the short-
comings of democracy have not escaped my notice, yet nowhere have I
found another system with a comparable degree of success and respect for
human dignity.

~~Finally, it was my Christian faith that led me to recognize and~~ wherever possible alleviate the ~~spiritual and material~~ misery of others ~~At the same time,~~ there is nothing ~~more profoundly disturbing than the use of religious fanaticism for political ends, regardless of denomination.~~

~~Years of close association with international politics has undoubtedly dampened the initial idealism of my youth and shaken my belief~~ in ~~the inevitable~~ victory ~~of international solidarity. The folly of those in power has often proved stronger than the aspirations of the people.~~

~~Yet I am not without hope—and this hope grows, the more I have an opportunity, during my lectures, seminars and talks, to meet, not so much those who exercise power, but~~ the ~~citizens of this world, in particular the young. I am a firm believer in the emerging groundswell of the people and have confidence in their~~ silent ~~but intensive rejection of the politics of the past. None the less, world peace will not come about through marches, speeches and prayers~~ alone ~~but rather through those in power recognizing where the people's interests really~~ lie ~~Sooner or later, some measure of national sovereignty will have to be relinquished in the interests of a broader global community. The first steps were taken forty years ago with the founding of the~~ United ~~Nations; many more must follow.~~

Epilogue

In the late summer ~~of 1945,~~ on the outskirts of a small town to the south ~~of Vienna, my wife, my infant daughter Liselotte and~~ I ~~stood before the gutted remains of my parents' house. The war was over at last and, after countless trials and tribulations, we refugees had found our way home from the Austrian Alps. Our quest, however, was not yet over: we sought not only our parents but also a roof over our heads.~~

~~The appearance of my parents' house dashed all our hopes: a ruin scorched by fire with the wind whistling at will through the broken window-panes. Utterly dejected and in silence we crept around the garden to the back, convinced that nobody could be living within the shattered walls—until suddenly we heard voices, and a door opened. Within seconds we were being~~ embraced ~~by my father and mother: both had survived the war.~~

~~Forty years have passed since that day, which, after years of dictatorship and military service, marked for me the start to~~ a new ~~life a life that at the outset had been filled with insecurity and anxiety about our future—a life that had also been marked by tragic events and experiences that were to determine my future thoughts and actions.~~

~~Many years later, after I had been elected by the United Nations to the highest office that the international community can bestow, I was repeatedly asked: where—behind all the impartiality of the office—were my real roots? Which principles had governed my life and~~ work ~~What had guided me along the lonely path through the undergrowth of ideologies and vested interests?~~

~~Like all essential questions no simple answer can be given. In retrospect however I feel that certain decisive influences can be traced: the history of Europe, my continent, and Austria, my homeland; my bitter experience of war; my study of law and my diplomatic career; as well as my~~

~~belief in democracy and the tenets of Christianity. Together they helped me to observe the claims of my conscience amidst all the different and often conflicting advice submitted by my international advisers.~~

It was ~~the tragic involvement of Europe in two world wars that~~ engendered in ~~me—as in so many of its citizens, the hope that national power politics could be overcome, and gave birth to~~ my dream ~~of a supra-national world government.~~

It was ~~Austria's indefatigable will to recover, and its active policy of neutrality, which showed me and my countrymen what solidarity and hard work can achieve and how bridges can be~~ built ~~between neighbours, however different their ideological concepts might be.~~

~~It was the war, with its hecatombs~~ of ~~innocent victims and ravages of minds and material, that convinced me of just how much men and women all over the world cherish one common~~ desire ~~peace and security for themselves and their children.~~

~~It was my study of law that brought home to me the degree to which a peaceful family of nations is dependent upon the existence and observance of mutually accepted norms as well as upon an international mechanism for solving conflict.~~

~~It was in my diplomatic career, through which I had always hoped to contribute in some small way to furthering understanding between peoples and nations, that I learnt to overcome distrust and scepticism through personal contacts and patient dialogue free of all emotion.~~

~~It was allegiance to democracy, tempered by the~~ experience ~~of fascism, which~~ taught me that in the final analysis ~~nothing is weaker than dictatorship. During my countless journeys around the globe the short-comings of democracy have not escaped my notice, yet nowhere have I found another system with a comparable degree of success and respect for human dignity.~~

~~Finally, it was my Christian faith that led me to recognize and, wherever possible, alleviate the spiritual and material misery of others. At the same time, there is~~ nothing ~~more profoundly disturbing than the use of religious fanaticism for political~~ ends ~~regardless of denomination.~~

~~Years of close association with international politics has undoubtedly dampened the initial idealism of my youth and shaken my belief in the inevitable victory of international solidarity. The folly of those in power has often proved stronger than the aspirations of the people.~~

~~Yet I am not without hope—and this hope grows, the more I have an opportunity, during my lectures, seminars and talks, to meet, not so much those who exercise power, but the citizens of this world, in particular the young. I am a firm believer in the emerging groundswell of the people and have confidence in their silent but intensive rejection of the politics of the past. None the less, world peace will not come about through marches, speeches and prayers alone, but rather through those in power recognizing where the people's interests really lie. Sooner or later, some measure of national sovereignty will have to be relinquished in the interests of a broader global community.~~ The first steps ~~were taken forty years ago with the founding of the United Nations; many more~~ must follow.

Epilogue

~~In the late summer of 1945, on the outskirts of a small town to the south of Vienna, my wife, my infant daughter Liselotte and~~ I stood before the ~~gutted~~ remains of ~~my parents' house. The war~~ was ~~over at last and, after countless trials and tribulations, we refugees had found our way home from the Austrian Alps. Our quest, however, was not yet over: we sought not only our parents but also a roof over our heads.~~

~~The appearance of my parents' house dashed all our hopes: a ruin scorched by fire with the wind~~ whistling ~~at will through the broken window-panes. Utterly dejected and in silence we crept around the garden to the back, convinced that nobody could be living within the shattered walls~~ — until ~~suddenly we heard voices, and~~ a door opened Within ~~seconds we were being embraced by~~ my ~~father and mother: both had survived the war.~~

~~Forty years have passed since that day, which, after years of dictatorship and military service, marked for me the start to a new~~ life ~~a life that at the outset had been filled with insecurity and anxiety about our future—a life that had also been marked by tragic events and experiences that were to determine my future thoughts and actions.~~

~~Many years later, after I had been elected by the United Nations to the highest office that the international community can bestow, I was repeatedly asked: where—behind all the impartiality of the office—were~~ my ~~real roots? Which principles had governed~~ my ~~life and work?~~ What ~~had~~ guided me ~~along the lonely path~~ through ~~the undergrowth of ideologies and vested interests?~~

~~Like all essential questions~~ no ~~simple~~ answer can be given ~~In retrospect~~ however I feel ~~that certain decisive influences can be traced: the history of Europe, my continent, and Austria, my homeland; my bitter experience of war; my~~ study of ~~law and my diplomatic career; as well as my~~

~~belief in democracy and the tenets of Christianity. Together they helped me to observe the claims of my~~ conscience ~~amidst all the different and often conflicting advice submitted by my international advisers.~~

~~It was the tragic involvement of Europe in two world wars that~~ engendered in me ~~as in so many of its citizens, the hope~~ that ~~national power politics could be overcome, and gave birth to my~~ dream ~~of a supra-national world government.~~

~~It was Austria's indefatigable will to recover, and its active policy of neutrality,~~ which showed me ~~and my countrymen what solidarity and hard work can achieve and how bridges can be built between neighbours, however different their ideological concepts might be.~~

~~It was the war, with its hecatombs of innocent victims and ravages of minds and material, that convinced me of just how much men and women all over the world cherish one common desire: peace and security for themselves and their children.~~

~~It was my study of law that brought home to me the degree to which~~ a ~~peaceful family of nations is dependent upon the existence and observance of mutually accepted norms as well as upon an international mechanism for solving conflict.~~

~~It was in my diplomatic career, through which I had always hoped to contribute in some~~ small ~~way to furthering understanding between peoples and nations, that I learnt to overcome distrust and scepticism through personal contacts and patient dialogue free of all emotion.~~

~~It was allegiance to democracy,~~ tempered ~~by the experience of fascism, which taught me that in the final analysis nothing is weaker than dictatorship. During my countless journeys around the~~ globe ~~the short-comings of democracy have not escaped my notice, yet~~ nowhere have I found another ~~system with a comparable degree~~ of ~~success and respect for human dignity.~~

~~Finally, it was my Christian faith~~ that ~~led me to recognize and, wherever possible, alleviate the spiritual and~~ material ~~misery of others. At the same time,~~ there is nothing ~~more profoundly disturbing than the use of religious fanaticism for political ends, regardless of denomination.~~

~~Years of close association with international politics has undoubtedly dampened the initial idealism of my youth and shaken my belief in the inevitable victory of international solidarity. The folly of those in power has often proved~~ stronger ~~than the aspirations of the people.~~

Yet I am not without hope ~~—and this hope grows, the more I have an opportunity, during my lectures, seminars and talks, to meet, not so much those who exercise power, but the~~ citizens ~~of this world, in particular the young.~~ I am a ~~firm~~ believer in ~~the emerging groundswell of the people and have confidence in their~~ silent ~~but intensive rejection of the politics of the past. None the less, world peace will not come about through marches, speeches and~~ prayers ~~alone, but rather through those in power recognizing where the people's interests really lie. Sooner or later, some measure of national sovereignty will have to be~~ relinquished ~~in the interests of a broader global community. The first steps were taken forty years ago with the founding of the United Nations; many more must follow.~~

Acknowledgments

Acknowledgment is due to the late Kurt Waldheim, whose English-language memoir, *In the Eye of the Storm,* originated this work. (Illustrations of the literary procedure underlying *Voyager* may be viewed at tiny.cc/voyagermethod). I am grateful to the editors of the following journals in which excerpts from this book, often in earlier versions, have appeared: *Black Clock, The Canary, Coconut, The Columbia Poetry Review, Crazyhorse, Critical Quarterly, The Denver Quarterly, Fence, The Indiana Review, The Iowa Review, jubilat, Lana Turner, Parcel, Poetry Northwest, A Public Space, Quarterly West, Witness,* and *The Canarium Anthology.* A previous draft of Book Two appeared, in its entirety, in *1913: A Journal of Forms;* and an earlier configuration of Book One was first published as a chapbook by Delirium Press of Montreal. My sincere thanks as well to the teachers, colleagues, friends, and family who lent support and guidance throughout the writing of this book. In all matters of art (and of the heart) the last word belongs to Suzanne.

NEW CALIFORNIA POETRY

edited by	Robert Hass
	Calvin Bedient
	Brenda Hillman
	Forrest Gander

Text and display Garamond Premier Pro
Compositor BookMatters, Berkeley
Printer and binder Maple-Vail Book Manufacturing Group